HELPING CHILDREN DEAL WITH BULLYING

Jenny Mosley and Helen Sonnet

Permission to photocopy

The rights of Jenny Mosley and Helen Sonnet to be identified as the authors of this work have
been asserted by them in accordance with sections 77 and 78 of the Copyright, Designs and Patents
Act 1988.

Helping Children Deal with Bullying
MT10012
ISBN-13: 978 1 85503 409 9
ISBN-10: 1 85503 409 3
© Jenny Mosley and Helen Sonnet
Illustrations © Gemma Hastilow
All rights reserved
First published 2006

Printed in the UK for LDA
Abbeygate House, East Road, Cambridge, CB1 1DB, UK

CONTENTS

INTRODUCTION

No school can say that it is free of bullying. It is an on-going problem that affects all schools at some stage. However, research has shown that effective intervention dramatically reduces its occurrence and impact.

In this book we have focused on what a school can do to help children deal with bullying. From the outset, it is important to say that if the adults in the school are not aware of their own behaviour, they may be contributing negatively to the ethos of the school – by engaging in put-downs or unkind behaviour towards each other or the children. Self-awareness amongst staff is one of the fundamental elements of a successful anti-bullying policy.

For the purpose of this concise book we shall assume that the staff in your school are working on their personal growth, self-awareness and relationships with each other and the children, and that they are actively committed to creating an ethos in which anti-bullying strategies can flourish.

This book highlights how, in such an atmosphere, schools can create an all-pervading, respectful anti-bullying ethos through systematic interventions with consistent consequences. Within this book there are strategies on how to interact effectively with children who bully, and information about the kind of response to expect from them as they progress towards a clearer understanding of their behaviour and its effects on others.

This book also focuses on how to help children who are being bullied, and explores the possibility that some advice is not appropriate. It offers guidance on how to encourage the support of parents and how to work with them as a team in a non-judgemental way.

You will learn how to have a positive influence on the large percentage of children who are not involved in bullying and who are of great significance in any anti-bullying campaign.

Importantly, this book supports the 'Say no to bullying' theme contained in the 2005 DfES publication *Excellence and Enjoyment: Social and Emotional Aspects of Learning* (SEAL).

WHAT IS BULLYING?

You will be familiar with the term 'bullying', but do you feel confident that you can distinguish bullying from other inappropriate behaviours? Look through the list on page 6 and tick any actions that you consider constitute bullying.

ACTION PLAN

Show members of staff the list of behaviours on page 6 and ask them to tick any that they would consider to be bullying. Ask them to add any other bullying behaviours they have witnessed to the bottom of the list.

ACTION PLAN

Look at your list of behaviours again, and discuss the factors that may make it clear whether the incidents described are bullying or not. From this, you can generate a definition of bullying to be used by staff and children as they explore this issue. The definition that you come up with should reflect the factors set out on page 7. Record your definition of bullying as part of your anti-bullying policy. Make sure that all members of your school community are aware of it – staff, governors, children and parents.

As you review this activity together, it should become clear that all of the behaviours listed can be types of bullying, depending on factors such as frequency, systematic nature and intent.

Having established that a range of behaviours can be seen as bullying, it is helpful to have a working definition of bullying in order to proceed from an agreed basis as your school develops ways of addressing this issue.

INAPPROPRIATE BEHAVIOURS

Tick the behaviours that you consider are types of bullying.

Spreading nasty rumours about several children ☐

Making a racist, sexist or homophobic remark ☐

Calling someone an unkind name ☐

Whispering about someone in front of them ☐

Using put-downs, sarcasm and insults ☐

Humiliating or excluding someone from a game ☐

Threatening to hurt someone ☐

Persistently blackmailing someone ☐

Using graffiti, e-mails, a website or text messages to communicate about someone ☐

Threatening to damage someone's property ☐

Hiding or stealing someone's property ☐

Physically hurting someone at playtime ☐

Demanding things from someone by force ☐

Suggesting someone is untouchable to another child ☐

Trying to persuade others to gang up on someone ☐

Bullying is generally accepted as having the following features:

1. It is a deliberate action – the desire to hurt someone is intentional rather than accidental.

2. It is unfair – the person/people doing the bullying is/are stronger, more powerful or has/have a higher status than the target of the bullying.

3. It is repeated over time – it is not a one-off incident of aggression or conflict.

Bullying may be divided into two main categories:

1. Physical – punching, kicking, hitting, hair pulling, twisting arms, tripping up.

2. Emotional – spreading malicious rumours, teasing, calling names, blackmailing, making offensive comments, ostracising, using put-downs, humiliating, making threats, embarrassing, excluding from activities.

Bullying may be direct, as in name-calling, teasing and physically hurting; or indirect, as in ostracising someone, spreading malicious rumours, making unpleasant comments, and giving scornful or dismissive glances.

REFLECT

What do you consider to be the most prevalent form of bullying in your school?

Do you sometimes overlook the less overt forms of bullying, concentrating on the more obvious examples?

Why does bullying happen?

There are many complex reasons why a child or children may bully another. Some of these are listed below. It may be:

- through an instinctive, personal dislike of someone;

- because it seems fun;

- to gain kudos or prestige with peers;

- to experience a feeling of power over others;

- to get something that they want;

- through jealousy of another person;

- to be in with a certain group;

- to avoid being bullied or as a result of being bullied;

- due to poor parenting and a lack of good role models;

- to cover up the way they feel;

- through lack of empathy for others;

- through feelings of exclusion.

Bullying is an inappropriate attempt to solve a problem or fulfil a need. It is not an inherent character trait; though some children are naturally more aggressive, this should not be automatically labelled as bullying. It is best to avoid labelling children involved in a bullying incident. Using the labels 'bully' and 'victim' may convey a feeling of permanence to the child concerned. This may be avoided by using terms such as 'the child who is bullied' and 'the child doing the bullying'.

ACTION PLAN

Talk through with the staff of your school the list of reasons why children may bully, to see which reasons may apply to children with whom they work.

How to prevent bullying

Bullying is a widespread problem and a source of worry for most schools, but research in the DfES SEAL materials has shown that with a focused, proactive approach it can be significantly reduced. Dealing with the child doing the bullying on their own or trying to teach assertiveness skills to counter bullying is not enough, and rarely brings long-term success.

Bullying will not flourish in an environment that actively promotes positive relationships and that has a proactive anti-bullying policy – lack of intervention tells those that bully and the targets of their bullying that this is an acceptable form of behaviour. A lack of action is a granting of permission.

The greatest impact on bullying comes from a whole-school approach in a co-ordinated campaign conducted over one or two terms, and revisited on a yearly basis. This needs to be supported by a consistent whole-school approach to promoting positive behaviour. We advocate using the Whole School Quality Circle Time model (for details of books and materials about this, see the Resources section at the end of the book). Using this model, the ethos of the school can be changed, which will have a greater impact than dealing with each incident as it occurs. A well-planned and purposeful programme will provide the challenge needed to raise every child's enthusiasm, encourage their ownership of your anti-bullying policy, and show that you take the issue seriously.

The important people to reach in any campaign to reduce bullying are the bystanders and witnesses. These are the children who are not actively involved in systematic bullying behaviour and are not the target of bullying. If their attitude and reactions are changed, bullying will be significantly reduced. They can have a positive influence on those already involved in bullying and those who may become involved. As a whole school, you can help children in the following ways:

- Implementing a whole-school proactive approach to anti-bullying. We suggest that this is done through the use of Quality Circle Time, Golden Rules and appropriate rewards and sanctions.

- Ensuring that your policy on bullying is explicit and that you initiate consistent intervention through a set of escalating consequences.

- Holding a campaign over at least one term to spread your anti-bullying message to all children. This could coincide with the Anti-Bullying Alliance's anti-bullying week, which is usually in November (www.anti-bullyingalliance.org). We have included other websites that you may find useful in the Resources section.

- Providing thoughtful and challenging scenarios, stories and role plays during assemblies and in class that will challenge the children's perceptions, and capture their imagination and enthusiasm.

- Gradually instilling an ethos into your school that encourages all the children to take responsibility for reporting bullying incidents that they may witness.

- Adopting a whole-school attitude that takes pride in the safe-school environment that you are able to offer – make sure that this pride rubs off onto the children.

- Encouraging parents to be party to and take pride in your safe-school policy through letters home, assemblies and conversations with them.

- Reviewing your procedures and attitudes regularly to maintain the standards necessary for success.

ACTION PLAN

Explore the anti-bullying websites in the Resources section for further advice and support as you prepare to consolidate and develop the work on this issue in your school.

At the onset of a programme relating to bullying, it is not unusual for there to be an increase in the number of incidents reported. Don't panic. As the work progresses and begins to have an impact on the children, there will be a gradual decline.

CREATING A SAFE SCHOOL ENVIRONMENT

The following five-strand programme will guide you through the procedure necessary to create a safer school environment for all your children. These strands are not stages that have to be worked through one after the other, but are discrete areas within the overall programme.

STRAND 1 – whole-school involvement

The first task is to review your existing anti-bullying policy document to check if it is comprehensive and effective. Involve as many members of the school community as possible in this process. If you do not have an anti-bullying policy, establish a working party involving a cross-section of the school community in order to develop one. All schools were sent the DfES anti-bullying charter, *Bullying – Don't Suffer in Silence*, in 2003. This included advice on what should be in an anti-bullying policy. As you prepare or review your policy, ask yourself the following questions:

1. Have all members of the school community – including children, governors, parents, lunchtime supervisors, teaching assistants and other ancillary staff – been involved in drawing up the policy document and agreeing on appropriate and inappropriate practice within their own roles?

2. Is there a clear definition of bullying?

3. Are the aims and objectives of the policy clearly stated at the beginning?

4. Are the strategies for addressing bullying that are set out in the policy document backed up by systems to ensure effective implementation?

5. Are there clear procedures regarding whom children should talk to, how they should respond and what follow-up is required?

6. Are all members of the school community familiar with all the types of bullying that may occur on the school premises?

7. Are all members of the school community familiar with the written procedures to follow in the event of a bullying incident and where to find them?

8. Is the senior management team's role of providing strong, consistent leadership in dealing with bullying explained?

9. Is there a strategy for promoting the anti-bullying message regularly through assemblies, whole-school and class events?

10. Are all incidents followed up with staff action to remind pupils that bullying is unacceptable and will not be tolerated in school?

REFLECT

Think about the vulnerable children in your school. Does your anti-bullying policy help directly to make their lives more comfortable and enjoyable? If not, what needs to be done to rectify the matter?

Implementation of consequences needs to be easy and not overly time consuming (see pages 34–37); otherwise staff may be tempted to turn a blind eye to incidents.

Once you have produced or revised your anti-bullying policy, make it available to all members of the school community, both adults and children. You will need to appoint a member of staff to be responsible for monitoring the effectiveness of the policy and providing regular updates on developments to the school community, so that it does not fade into the background.

Your policy should be in line with the school's behaviour policy. It should be reviewed on a regular basis, at least once every school year.

An assembly

At the start of a focus on bullying, introduce the topic through a whole-school assembly. Explain to the children that you are going to tell them a story, and that you want them to listen very carefully as you will be asking them for helpful ideas afterwards. You can use the following story or one that is specifically tailored to your school's particular needs and age group. See Excellence and Enjoyment: Social and Emotional Aspects of Learning (DfES, 2005) for some useful assemblies.

Ryan and his friends always picked on Sophie. They called her unkind names and made faces at her if she looked at them. Sometimes they accidentally-on-purpose knocked her pencil or books off the table onto the floor. They pushed and jostled her when lining up and even punched her when the teacher wasn't looking. They had, once or twice, taken her break-time snack out of her drawer and thrown it into the rubbish bin. If they had to work in a group with Sophie, they made nasty comments and refused to sit or stand next to her. Occasionally, Sophie said something back to them, telling them how mean they were, but it didn't make things better. At playtimes, Sophie always stood next to the teacher on duty. She was too scared to move away in case Ryan and his friends started to pick on her. She became very sad and anxious about going to school and was often away ill.

After reading the story to the children, ask questions to explore aspects of it. You could record their answers on a flipchart for later use. For the story above, you could use the following:

- How do you think Sophie felt about Ryan and his friends?

- If they did know what was happening, what could other children have done to improve the situation?

- In the story nobody told the teacher about what was going on. Why do you think nobody did?

- What would make it easier to tell a teacher if someone was being bullied?

- How could we make our school a safe place for everyone?

After exploring suggestions, continue:

This term we are looking at ways of making our school safe for all the children in it. This assembly is part of that work, and there will be a lot of interesting things to follow. Can you think how we could give our story a happy ending?

Once you have listened to some suggestions, if you have used the story on page 11 you could share the following ending with the children, asking them how similar it is to their suggestions.

Some children didn't like the way Ryan and his friends treated Sophie. They decided to tell their teacher about it. This was brave of them as they were worried that Ryan might pick on them instead. They waited for a time when everyone else was out of the classroom, then approached their teacher. She listened to what they had to say and thanked them for telling her.

The teacher then talked and listened to Sophie and, finally, had a long talk to Ryan and his friends. She encouraged them to think about their actions – why they did them and how they made Sophie feel. She talked to them regularly, every week, reminding them how to be kind, and she talked to all the other children in the class as well, urging them to report any incidents of bullying. She explained how this could be done in confidence, so that no-one else need know. She also asked them to nominate children for kind actions. They were encouraged to nominate children who were not their close friends. The class did a Circle Time to help each other to be kind and considerate, and after a while the incidents of people being picked on started to fall, until they were very rare indeed. Everyone in the class was happier – particularly Sophie, who stopped being anxious about going to school.

Tell the children that they will be doing projects on making their school a safer place for everyone, and it would be a good idea to think beforehand about how they might achieve this. Encourage them to talk about their ideas amongst themselves so they can take their suggestions to a Circle Time in their class.

Introduce the class Circle Time suggestion boxes in which children can post ideas anonymously. This could be a decorated box with a slot cut in it. The box is opened by the teacher before the special Circle Time and the suggestions are read and brought to the circle. Some schools have similar boxes for children to post reports on bullying in.

REFLECT

Most people experience bullying at some time in their life. Think about your own experience of this, how it made you feel and how it was resolved or came to an end.

Useful whole-school strategies

- Organise an in-service training day for the teaching staff before initiating your anti-bullying programme, in order to dispel any myths that might be held about bullying. Look at the evidence to support your proposed approach. You could bring in an outside trainer to give the launch some impetus. Invite parents to come to a relevant part of the day, or organise an evening session at a later date for them. These events could explore the importance of tackling bullying, an empathic understanding of the experience of being bullied, a definition of bullying, the vocabulary of bullying and the development of the school's anti-bullying policy.

- Organise an in-service training morning/afternoon for lunchtime supervisors to look at all aspects of the programme that affect them. Make sure they understand the nature of the behaviours the school is classifying as bullying and know the correct procedures to follow after any incidents.

- Commission a survey to be carried out by each class to highlight the frequency, type and location (hot spots) of bullying within the school. This can be done by annotating a map of the school, using colours, pictures and words.

- Ensure that there is always adequate supervision by adults in areas that are highlighted as hot spots. Effective supervision of such areas by informed adults will have a big impact on the bullying within a school.

- In Circle Time teach non-aggressive strategies of conflict resolution and peer mediation to all children – see Resources for books and also the list of websites. Remember that these skills are not enough on their own. Children often find it difficult to implement them in bullying situations because they feel isolated. Within a supportive, proactive ethos, children feel more empowered to use these skills because there are frameworks in place and witnesses are more likely to react helpfully.

- Always treat reports of bullying as serious and follow them up with appropriate action, as outlined in your anti-bullying policy.

- Adopt a very public attitude towards bullying, showing the children that intervention in some form will always take place.

- Display posters around the school to remind children of the school's policy towards bullying and to keep its profile high.

- Talk to the children frequently about the strategies and words they can use if they are bullied or if they see others being bullied.

- Teach the children a class rhyme that reinforces the anti-bullying policy, such as the following:

Our class is caring; we want to make it clear

Our attitude is totally 'No bullying' in here.

Our class is caring; we have a sense of calm,

One where we show tolerance and no-one comes to harm.

Our class is caring; we all know the rule

That every single person should feel safe in school.

Practise this rhyme with your class until they know it by heart. You could display a copy to use for reference. The children could devise their own verses to share with the group.

Whole-school playtime policy

In primary schools, most bullying occurs in the playground. Your whole school needs to be actively engaged with a positive playtime policy. The following ideas will help you start.

Ask the children and lunchtime staff for their ideas on how to make the playground a safer place for everyone. Use these as the basis for further discussion and the preparation of an action plan to tackle such issues, including short- and long-term goals. Share this with the school community and review it regularly to assess progress. The school community will be much more motivated about fund-raising to pay for improvements if they see progress and feel a sense of momentum.

Look at issues such as the adequate policing of trouble spots, introducing more and varied activities to combat boredom – such as hula hoops and organised group games. This will have a positive impact on the amount of bullying that takes place in the playground.

Consider creating designated areas for various activities, including a quiet area where children can sit and read or relax.

Devise a system that involves the children in monitoring and preventing incidents in the playground. We create a group called Playground Friends to do this work. They care for children who are lonely and on the margins – the sorts of children who may experience bullying. Playground Friends will be good role models for any witnesses to bullying incidents as they tell the child doing the bullying to stop, lead the child being bullied to a safe place, and find an adult and tell them what is happening. Stress that it is not the Friend's role to sort out any problems. The Playground Friend requires the maturity to know when to seek the help of an adult and not to exceed their brief.

You could pair a younger, vulnerable child with an older Playground Friend. If the younger child feels threatened, they can go and stand with their older friend.

See Mosley and Thorp, *Positive Playtimes* (2005) in the Resources section for more ideas on creating safer playtimes.

STRAND 2 – helping the class deal with bullying

Make sure that your incentives and sanctions work. Using Golden Rules that outline the moral code of your school and Golden Time, an inclusive rewards procedure, is effective. The rigour of any rewards and sanctions system must be maintained. A positive ethos can diminish quickly if it is not monitored, reviewed and reinforced. Positive behaviour, such as being kind and caring to others, should be mentioned frequently in the classroom to remind children how they should behave.

You might like to display a charter that states the good intentions you would like all the children to adopt, asking them to sign it to show their willingness to participate (see page 16). Remind them from time to time of the content, especially if behaviour is starting to deteriorate and there is an increase in bullying.

Weekly Circle Times

A regular weekly Circle Time helps combat bullying for the following reasons:

ACTION PLAN

Ask the children to design anti-bullying leaflets outlining the positive ethos of the school and its anti-bullying stance to take home to their parents.

- It pulls the class together into a caring team.

- It encourages children not to name one another in a negative way.

- It promotes and rewards positivity.

- It keeps kindness high on the agenda.

- It teaches children ground rules for good behaviour.

- It gives children the appropriate language for negotiation.

- It provides children with the opportunity to practise discussing issues in a non-blaming way.

- It helps to raise children's self-esteem.

- It provides an opportunity for all children to be valued equally.

- It enhances children's social skills.

- It encourages children to speak and to listen effectively.

CLASSROOM CHARTER

We, the children of

-- class
believe that all the members of our class have a right
to feel safe in school.

We agree to be kind to one another and to all the children in our
school, and to consider their feelings in the way we behave.

We will try not to hurt anyone with unkind actions or words.
Signed:

--------------------------------------   --------------------------------------

--------------------------------------   --------------------------------------

--------------------------------------   --------------------------------------

--------------------------------------   --------------------------------------

--------------------------------------   --------------------------------------

--------------------------------------   --------------------------------------

--------------------------------------   --------------------------------------

--------------------------------------   --------------------------------------

--------------------------------------   --------------------------------------

--------------------------------------   --------------------------------------

--------------------------------------   --------------------------------------

--------------------------------------   --------------------------------------

--------------------------------------   --------------------------------------

© Helping Children Deal with Bullying LDA   Permission to Photocopy

In order to conduct the Circle Times on pages 19–27 effectively, you need a thorough understanding of the stages involved in a Circle Time, within the Quality Circle Time model. They are as follows.

Meeting up – playing a game

Begin a Circle Time with an enjoyable, pacy – but not too energetic – warm-up activity or game. This helps the children to relax and enjoy being together. It is a good idea to play a game that involves the children changing places so that they are not necessarily sitting next to their close friends. This gives them the opportunity to make new friends and helps to build group identity.

Warming up – breaking the silence

This step is designed to remind children that they all have the right to speak and the responsibility to listen during Circle Time. This involves a quick round in which the leader introduces a simple sentence stem such as 'My favourite colour is . . .'. The person on the leader's right repeats this stem, completing it with their favourite colour. This continues round the circle until it gets back to the leader, who completes the stem for themselves. Further rounds can be played if needed.

A speaking object is used to show whose turn it is to speak. Whoever is holding it has the right to speak without interruption. They pass the speaking object to the next person after they have said their sentence. The speaking object needs to be small enough to fit into a child's hands: a painted wooden egg, a small soft toy or a suitable object linked to your current topic all work well.

> **REFLECT**
>
> *Is your Circle Time as regular and effective as it could be? There are excellent books available to help you deliver an effective programme (see Resources).*

Holding the speaking object does not oblige anyone to speak; any child who does not wish to do so may say 'pass' and hand it on. Some children often say 'pass' because they don't have the confidence to speak or they are testing the teacher. Aim to tell the children the day before the Circle Time what the round is going to be about, and give them a chance to think about their sentence – they can even write it down on a small card. If a child finds it difficult to prepare, you may need to give them a little help in advance. Very young children may be shy, and it is a good idea to conduct a series of smaller circles before the main Circle Time, with a puppet who chats to the children about what will happen in the main Circle Time and offers to speak for any child who feels shy. A child can tell the puppet their sentence before the main Circle Time begins and the puppet will repeat their sentence at the appropriate time.

Opening up – exploring issues that concern the class

Now that the children are relaxed and have practised speaking and listening, they are ready to tackle the most challenging phase of the Circle Time. This is called 'open forum' and is an opportunity to express opinions and discuss important issues. This middle phase encourages children to develop a belief in their ability to make responsible choices and decisions, an essential part of any anti-bullying programme. Problem-solving skills can be rehearsed and targets can be agreed. Children should remember to raise their hands or make a thumbs-up gesture before speaking, speak one at a time and listen to each other.

The use of metaphor to help children discuss difficult issues is a useful part of this Circle Time phase – stories, role play, puppets and dressing up can be used to help them explore problems, concerns, hopes or fears.

Cheering up – celebrating the positive

Before a Circle Time concludes, it is important to bring the discussion phase of the meeting to an end. The cheering-up phase is used to celebrate the group's successes and strengths and give praise and thanks to one another. This may be immediate praise for the work done in the meeting, or a general celebration of recent school accomplishments. This step makes them feel more competent, happy and positive. This is a good time to acknowledge the successes of the anti-bullying programme so far and to keep it fresh and vibrant in the children's minds.

Calming down – bridging

It is crucial that children experience quiet and calm before they leave the circle. This activity is called 'bridging'. A closing ritual enables the transition to the next part of the day to be smooth and successful. You could play a very calm game, such as passing the tambourine round the circle without its making a sound. Alternatively, a guided visualisation, listening to a rainstick or some calming music can be used. In such ways, you touch the children's imagination and allow the events of the Circle Time to sink in.

These five phases are the building blocks of the Quality Circle Time model.

The following Circle-Time scripts explore aspects of bullying. We have concentrated on the open forum section in order to give detailed guidance on how this phase of Circle Time can be used to help children deal with bullying. The open forum stage is the heart of a Circle Time, in which difficult issues are explored in a space that is emotionally safe.

What is bullying?

Photocopy pages 20 and 21 so you have one of each between two. Put the children in pairs round the circle and give each pair a copy of page 20.

Ask the children to look through the incidents on the sheet and discuss which ones they think show bullying. The children need to tick those that they think show bullying behaviour. Allow five minutes for this, and then go round the circle asking each pair to share the letters of the incidents they ticked. Explore the reasons behind the children's choices.

A, C, D, E, G, I, J are potentially forms of bullying. B, F, H are arguments between children.

Discuss the reasons why some incidents are considered to be bullying. To do this, use the definition that follows, which should be the basis of the definition in your anti-bullying policy.

Bullying is generally accepted as having the following features:

1. It is a deliberate action – the desire to hurt someone is intentional rather than accidental.

2. It is unfair – the person/people doing the bullying is/are stronger, more powerful or has/have a higher status than the target of the bullying.

3. It is repeated over time – it is not a one-off incident of aggression or conflict.

Give each pair a copy of page 21. Tell the children to look carefully at all the characters in the illustration. If necessary, read out the

thought bubble of each character before asking the children to imagine how the target of the bullying is feeling. In turn, look at the bystanders in the illustration and discuss their thoughts and motives.

When discussing the children who are supporting the bullying, explore what the children think their hopes or fears are. Common answers include these:

- They admire the bully's power.

- They are scared of being bullied themselves.

- They think it's cool to be in the bully's gang.

Ask the children if they have ever witnessed a bullying incident. If so, ask them to explain what happened without naming any of the children involved. Ask them how they responded at the time, if they are willing to discuss this. What did they think and how did they feel about what happened? Did they do anything? If not, what prevented them from taking any action? For this to happen, you must make sure that you have established a non-judgemental ethos within your circle. Children need to feel that admitting their mistakes is not going to be held against them. Rather, it is an important part of the learning process for themselves and the group and will have a positive impact on the group and the school.

Explain to the children that telling an adult about a bullying incident is the right thing to do. Taking a collective responsibility is the best way to stop bullying.

WHAT IS BULLYING? ACTIVITY 1

Tick the incidents that you feel show bullying.

A Ben has taken Anya's pencil case and thrown it in the rubbish bin. ☐

B Charmaine and Dionne have fallen out over a piece of work they were doing together. During the argument, Dionne pushes Charmaine over. ☐

C Sam watches for Tom to go into the toilets, then follows him in and sprays him with water from the tap. ☐

D Natasha laughs with her friends about Zoe, commenting loudly that her clothes are not trendy. ☐

E Whenever Dylan puts his hand up to answer a question, Joe sniggers and makes comments under his breath like, 'Oh, thicko's bound to get it wrong again.' ☐

F The boys are playing football in the playground. A fight breaks out between Paul and Ashley over a disallowed goal. ☐

G Kayleigh tells her friends not to play with Rebecca because she doesn't like her. ☐

H Rashid shouts at his best friend Dan in a quarrel over a broken toy. ☐

I A group of boys make fun of Tariq every time he speaks because his English is not very good. ☐

J Every day in the playground, Katie and her friends corner Laura and demand that she gives them her snack. ☐

    Permission to Photocopy

Permission to Photocopy

What types of bullying are there?

During this open forum, you are going to explore the different forms that bullying can take. This draws on the categories mentioned earlier:

1. Physical – punching, kicking, hitting, hair pulling, twisting arms, tripping up.

2. Emotional – spreading malicious rumours, teasing, calling names, blackmailing, making offensive comments, ostracising, using put-downs, humiliating, making threats, embarrassing, excluding from activities.

You will need three different-coloured marker pens and some large sheets of paper stuck together. In the middle of the paper write 'Types of bullying' and draw a circle round it. In two separate smaller circles on the sheet, write one of each of the following types of bullying: emotional and physical. Join these circles to the main circle by drawing a line from each of them to it. Do all this with one of the marker pens, keeping the other two for later.

Now that you have your web diagram prepared, place it in the centre of the circle in readiness for the open forum. Explain to the children that bullying can take different forms and read out the two categories listed on the web diagram. Ask the children to tell you examples of bullying and say which category they think they belong in. Some of these examples will be direct bullying, such as punching, calling names and taking someone's

property; others will be indirect bullying, such as spreading rumours and ostracising someone.

Depending on the age of the group, you can either write the suggestions on the web diagram yourself or ask the children to do so. Whichever you decide, you need to do two things beforehand. Firstly, after a suggestion you need to discuss which category of bullying the example belongs to. Secondly, you need to decide whether the suggestion is an example of direct or indirect bullying. Once these things have been resolved, the suggestion can be written on the paper near the category it relates to. Choose one colour to write the suggestion if it is an example of direct bullying and the remaining colour if it is indirect bullying. Use the pen to draw a line to the category that the suggestion relates to.

As you gather suggestions, your web diagram will increase in complexity and become a record of the group's growing understanding of the issue. You will end up with a web diagram similar to that shown on page 23. This diagram can be used as a classroom display, with children being encouraged to think of further examples that could be added to the diagram over time. It could also be used as part of an assembly or an event involving parents, other children and staff members.

End the open forum with a round using the following sentence stem:

'One thing I have learnt about bullying today is . . .'

WEB DIAGRAM

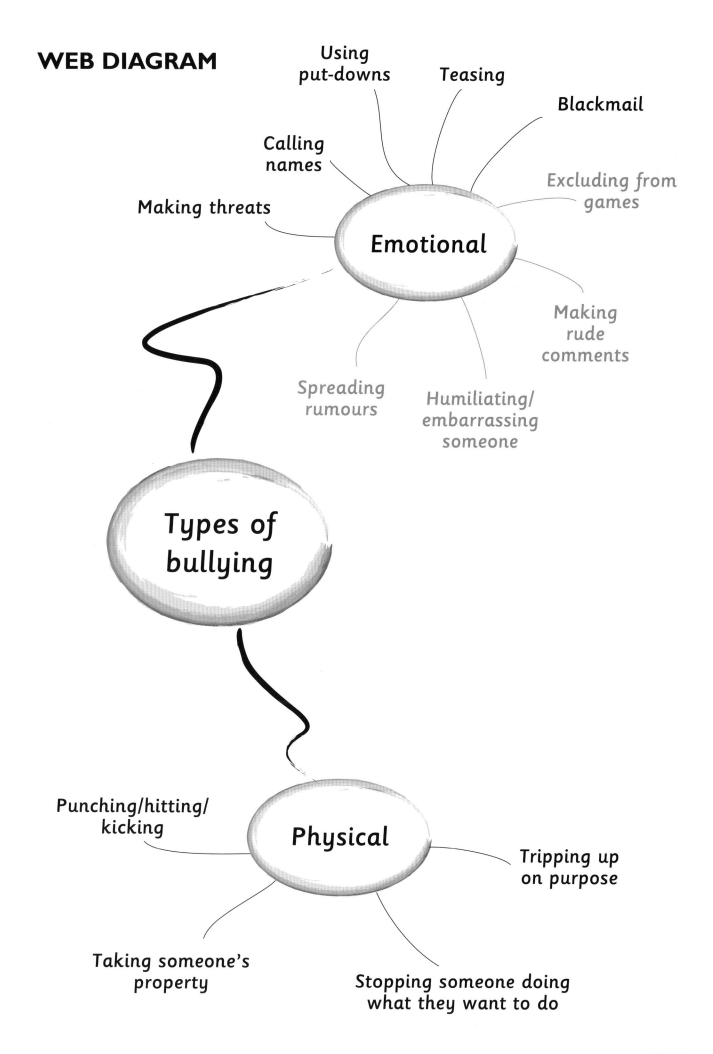

Using put-downs

Teasing

Blackmail

Calling names

Excluding from games

Making threats

Emotional

Making rude comments

Spreading rumours

Humiliating/ embarrassing someone

Types of bullying

Punching/hitting/ kicking

Physical

Tripping up on purpose

Taking someone's property

Stopping someone doing what they want to do

Permission to Photocopy

Is bullying ever OK?

Ask the children the question: 'Is bullying ever OK?' This needs to be asked in the spirit of exploration so that the children do not assume that you are looking for a 'no' answer. If they are unwilling to offer suggestions, you could make one or two of your own. The sorts of suggestions that you could make, or that may be offered, are as follows:

- To stop someone bullying you.

- If someone keeps hurting your friend.

- To get revenge on someone.

- Because other children do it.

- It's only a bit of fun.

- My mum/dad told me to give as good as I get.

Take some time to explore these suggestions and the potential problems associated with them, such as:

- you will get into trouble;

- your actions may escalate a situation;

- bullying creates an unhealthy atmosphere;

- someone may be hurt.

Ask the children how they feel inside when they have been mean to someone. Encourage the children to realise that bullying someone may give them a temporary feeling of revenge or power, but this will be replaced by a negative feeling, even though they may not acknowledge that to others.

Get them to contrast this with how good they feel when they have done something kind or generous. Ask the children to give you examples of things of this nature that they have done.

ACTION PLAN

Use the comments from the open forum as part of a presentation in an assembly to explore some of the things the children have learnt about bullying.

How could incidents of bullying be reported?

Ask the children why people don't always report incidents of bullying. Among the comments you will probably have these:

- 'I don't like to tell tales.'

- 'If I tell on someone, everyone might not like me.'

- 'I'm scared that the person doing the bullying will pick on me.'

- 'My friend is doing the bullying.'

- 'I don't like the person being bullied.'

- 'It's nothing to do with me.'

Remind the children that you have explored bullying, seen the upset that it causes, and agreed that it needs to be addressed. Explain that to do this and to create a physically and emotionally safe school, any incidents of bullying must be reported to an adult. Reassure children that reports will be treated with tact and, where appropriate, confidentiality.

Ask for suggestions about the best ways to achieve this. You could create a worry box for the classroom into which they can post notes to you regarding being bullied or bullying they have seen. You can read these notes and deal with any follow-up, reassuring the writers if the follow-up is not seen by them.

You could have a special time and place where children could meet with you to report incidents. We use a system called Bubble Time, a one-to-one listening system to provide a

time for private discussion between the teacher and pupils.

You could display the methods you have agreed as a notice in the classroom. Review this list from time to time to see if the systems are working and if they need to be changed or refined.

If you use a standard form such as the one on page 26 to record any incidents of bullying, it will be less time consuming for you to keep a record and easier to respond to an incident.

REFLECT

Are you treating reports of bullying seriously and making your follow-up and feedback clear? Your responses are crucial as far as the children's confidence in a change for the better is concerned.

FORM TO REPORT AN INCIDENT OF BULLYING

Date:. . . . .

Name of child/children doing the bullying: . . . .

Class(es): . . . .

Name of target of bullying: . . . .

Class: . . . .

Name of witness(es):. . . . .

Class(es):. . . . .

Nature of incident

Ring as appropriate.

Physical
Hitting
Kicking
Punching
Throwing objects
Stopping someone from doing something
Damaging someone's property

Emotional
Humiliating
Making nasty comments
Threatening
Spreading rumours
Stealing someone's property
Name-calling
Persuading others to leave someone out

Other: . . . .

Action taken: . . . .

. . . .

. . . .

Signed: . . . .

    Permission to Photocopy

The difference between telling tales and reporting bullying incidents

Remind the children that during the previous Circle Time you explored ways in which to report incidents of bullying. All the ways that you talked about involved disclosing the name of the child doing the bullying. Explain that it is important to be able to understand the difference between telling tales about someone and reporting bullying.

Read out the following statements and ask the children to think about whether each is a case of tale-telling or if bullying is being reported.

1. Ashad tells the teacher that Damon keeps hiding his work to try to get him into trouble.

2. Alicia tells the teacher that Mary is playing with a toy on the carpet during listening time.

3. Richard tells the teacher that Amy is saying nasty things about a new girl so that no-one will like her.

4. Helen tells the teacher that Daniel hasn't handed his work in as requested.

5. Dale tells the teacher that Leroy was playing with water at the sink.

6. Zoe tells the teacher that Cara has been calling Isabelle a nasty name during playtimes.

After some thinking time, read out each statement in turn and ask the children what they think about them. It should become clear that incidents 2, 4 and 5 are examples of telling tales. Explain that telling tales on someone occurs when their words or actions are not hurting anyone or endangering themselves.

ACTION PLAN

Do you have an adequate rewards and sanctions system in action in your classroom that diminishes the need to tell tales? If not, see Mosley and Sonnet, Better Behaviour through Golden Time (2005) in the Resources section.

Using role play in Circle Time to teach good practice

Put the children into groups of six and give each group one of the scenarios on page 28. You might want to write them out on index cards beforehand and read them out as you give one to each group. Ask the children to divide the roles in their scenario between the members of their group. Give the children five to ten minutes to practise acting out their scene, encouraging them to imagine how they would feel in their character's situation. Stress that if names are used, they should not be those of children they know. As they develop their role play, ask the children to work out how they would act, and what they might say and do. They must try to make their role play as realistic as possible. You could either allow the role plays to develop naturally or specify whether you want a positive, negative or mixed reaction from the bystanders.

> **1.** Two children are whispering and pointing at a third child, who is upset. Three other children see what is happening.
>
> **2.** One child has trapped another child against a wall and won't let them pass. Four other children are watching.
>
> **3.** A child has stolen another child's snack and won't give it back. Four bystanders are watching.
>
> **4.** Three children have ganged up on a fourth and are calling them unkind names. Two children are watching.
>
> **5.** One child is trying to persuade four others not to play with another child.

After the rehearsal time is up, ask each group in turn to show their role play to the rest of the class. You may be required to participate.

Learning from the role-play situations

After all of the groups have performed their role plays, discuss with the whole group the range of responses observed. Pay particular attention to the children who took the role of the bystanders. Bystanders play a crucial role in any anti-bullying programme, and in any bullying situation this is the individual or group that you want to act positively.

Focus on the role plays in which the bystanders took a positive approach. Perhaps they showed one of the following responses:

> **1.** They were brave and intervened directly, telling the child doing the bullying to stop. While this is a suitable reaction, it is one that is quite rare in reality.
>
> **2.** They intervened by leading the victim to a safe place – for example, by saying, 'Come on, we need you in our game.'
>
> **3.** They decided to find an adult and tell them what was happening.

REFLECT

Why does most bullying take place in front of witnesses? This is a question that you could explore with the children.

Bystanders often aid the person doing the bullying by their tacit approval of or interest in what is taking place. An important action that they can take is to show disapproval for bullying incidents. This is a message that needs repeating to remind children of the importance of this approach and the positive impact that it can have. It can be a major factor in creating a safe-school environment. Bystanders can exert peer pressure on any child involved in bullying and have a significant impact on the number of incidents of bullying that occur.

ACTION PLAN

Try setting up an acting scenario in the middle of the circle and freezing it at a certain point. Choose other children to join the action. They swap places with one of the characters by placing their hand on the participant's shoulder. They change places and continue the action with their own choice of dialogue. This adds additional depth and different dimensions to the action.

Developing empathy

In your anti-bullying programme, it is important to help children to develop empathy. There follows two examples of ways in which this can be achieved.

Poetry

Poetry is a good way to explore issues surrounding bullying and to help children connect with the underlying feelings of those who bully and the targets of bullying. The following short poem is a good way to begin this sort of work with children:

You'd better not be too fat, too thin or too tall;
You'd better not have big ears, a long nose or be small.
Don't be clever, slow or have a different view;
'Cos you don't want those that bully to notice you.

Ask the children to think of reasons why people might be picked on. Try to look at issues such as physical characteristics, wealth, race, sex, religion and mannerisms. An awareness of such issues is an important step for children negotiating them in their daily lives as their self-awareness develops.

Personal reflection

Ask the children to imagine that they are being bullied. You can make up a specific incident, such as being called unkind names, being excluded from games or having their belongings destroyed, or allow them to decide on the issue. Ask them to think very carefully about how they would feel.

You can use picture books, such as *Willy and Hugh* by Anthony Browne (Candlewick Press, 2003), to stimulate thinking. Puppets can also be used for this.

Invite the children to write a poem with the following beginning. Ask them to describe the items in square brackets.

I don't like going to school any more,
something horrid is happening there . . .
[What]
[How it makes me feel inside]
[What I wish would happen]

If the children are going to use names in their poems, ask them to use names that do not link anyone within their group to the incident.

Find a time to share some of these poems with the group and to explore the outcomes at the end of the poems. Discuss if they are realistic outcomes and if they are already part of the school's anti-bullying policy. If they are not, they could be passed on to the person responsible for the upkeep of the anti-bullying policy.

You could use the poems as part of a display or in an assembly.

Positively celebrating individual differences

In order to create a positive and caring dynamic within your class, it is important to celebrate every individual's uniqueness and promote tolerance of other people's differences.

It will help towards the latter if you hold a Circle Time exploring each other's differences. Play a game in which the children swap seats based on different categories (e.g. 'Swap seats if you . . . have black hair / blue eyes / a brother / a dog / like chicken). Encourage the children to understand that people are born with physical features and into a social setting that may be challenging. In other words, 'You are who you are.' As the children grasp this fact, they will begin to understand that everyone has a right to be accepted and valued.

REFLECT

Am I a good role model? Do I try to favour all the children in my class equally, letting them know that I see each of them as special?

You can extend this work on celebrating differences by working with the children on a display entitled 'All about me'. This can include a photograph of each child (you could use the school's digital camera, if it has one) and other information about themselves, such as:

One thing I enjoy doing is . . .
My favourite meal is . . .
I am good at . . .
My favourite lesson is . . .
When I am older I would like to be . . .

Creating positive group dynamics

In addition to encouraging tolerance and empathy, it is important to promote a positive group dynamic through team-building activities. If your class views itself in a positive way – seeing itself as a happy, caring, established group of children – there will not be the kind of negative atmosphere that will allow bullying to flourish. This self-fulfilling prophecy is absolutely true: telling your children on a regular basis that they are a super, kind, caring class will encourage them to become just that.

ACTION PLAN

Use other strategies to encourage kindness, such as a 'tree of kindness' display. Place a bare twig in a pot. Cut out leaf shapes. Each time a child is kind, they can write their name and action on a leaf and attach it to the tree. Watch the tree flourish!

Other group-building activities

Some useful books that contain group-building activities are listed in the Resources at the end of this book. The most effective activities to use are those that create a feel-good atmosphere and are non-competitive. Games that require co-operation and the pooling of resources are valuable for building trust and enhancing relationships. A child involved in bullying could work in a group of sensible, reliable children alongside a potential target of bullying. Away from the usual group of supporters, and with the guidance and encouragement of trustworthy children, the child involved in bullying can develop a more positive relationship with a target of bullying.

Some examples of suitable activities follow.

1. Ask the children to get into groups of five or six and devise a fun day out that all members of the group would enjoy. They must discuss the suggestions put forward by members of the group democratically until they are agreed on what the day will include. After ten minutes, ask each group to share their plans for the day with the rest of the class.

2. Ask the children to get into groups of five or six. Give each group a different task to mime that has a number of stages, such as going camping – which could involve putting up a tent, unpacking bedding and equipment, collecting water, cooking a meal. Ask each group to work on their mime, taking each stage at a time and devising something humorous that could happen during it. For example, the tent collapses, the sleeping bags roll down the hill, the water carrier has a hole in it, and the pancakes for tea get stuck in a tree when they are tossed. You may need to offer the groups some suggestions if they are stuck. Give each group ten minutes to rehearse their mime. After this time, ask each group to announce the theme of their mime and then perform it to the rest of the group.

3. Ask the children to get into groups of five or six. Give the groups a story starter, for example:

'One dark and stormy night, I was walking home when a creature leapt out from the bushes directly in front of me and ...'.

Tell the groups to find a space to work in, and to spend ten minutes talking quietly – so that they are not overheard – about what will happen next in their version of the story. They then decide how they are going to tell it to the group. After ten minutes, call the groups

ACTION PLAN

Ask the children to make eye-catching posters about how to make the classroom or playground safer.

back together and ask each group in turn to tell their story to the rest of the class. Discuss how the stories were different and yet no less valid or interesting because of this.

4. In a circle, play games that encourage the children to use each other's names. For example, begin with the children in the circle standing and ask one child to begin the action by greeting another child ('Hello, . . .') and then sitting down. All the children, whether sitting or standing, clap twice and the child named greets another standing child and so on, until the last person standing says 'Hello, everyone' and sits down.

5. Using a set of playing cards, sort out enough sets of four cards of the same value to cover the number in your group — you may need to have a group of two or three and join in yourself. Give each child a card. On your command, the children have to move about the playing area until they find the other children with the same value as them. When they do, they sit down. When all the groups are sitting down, take in the cards, shuffle them well and redistribute them to play another round.

6. Cut up five different pictures into six jigsaw pieces each. These could be magazine photographs or pictures from the Internet stuck onto card. Give each of the children in your class a jigsaw piece. If you have more or fewer than 30 children, adjust the jigsaws accordingly. Tell the children they must move around the playing area trying to find the children with the other pieces to complete their picture. Once they have found everyone, they sit down in their group and make their jigsaw.

STRAND 3 – working with a child involved in bullying

The most important thing to remember when you are working with children involved in bullying is that you cannot control the behaviour of others in a healthy way. However, with a carefully planned programme, you can make positive behaviour appear more rewarding than negative behaviour and encourage a child to change. The tips that follow will help you to accomplish this:

- Try to understand the factors in the life of the child doing the bullying that have helped them to stay afloat and that may make it difficult for them to change.

- Understand that changing behaviour is hugely difficult for all of us – behaviour patterns may have become established over many years.

- Don't expect behaviour to change overnight – it is a slow and gradual process, often in very small steps.

- Don't ever label the child as naughty, stupid, or a bully – person-oriented criticism creates helplessness and a feeling that they are unable to change. Base your criticism on the child's actions; for example, say 'Pushing the chair over was an unkind thing to do' rather than 'You are a very unkind child.'

- Don't over-react to lapses – you will make the child doubt their ability to change.

- Keep going with your encouragement over time – one week's intensive focus is not enough.

Setting up a support programme

The most effective way of helping a child involved in bullying to change their behaviour is through a two-pronged approach:

I. Enforce inevitable and predictable consequences for bullying behaviour.

2. Reward positive behaviour.

The consequences

Providing a set of predictable and escalating sanctions that are applicable to the whole school community is an important part of a successful anti-bullying programme. Such a system provides for consistent and inevitable actions, rather than arbitrary responses based on an individual adult's views, personality, mood at the time or feelings towards the child. Sanctions should be discussed with members of the school staff and agreed as the basis for dealing with difficult behaviour and bullying. All children should be made aware of the agreed system so that there is no confusion regarding the consequences of their actions.

Inevitable consequences ensure that adults are not discriminatory in their responses – handing out lighter punishments to good students for the same offence is seen as unfair by other children. Children need to know what the consequence of their behaviour will be. This makes it more likely that they will own up to their offences. Predictable consequences help teachers and save time as consulting a list or document where they are recorded shows them what response to make.

We advocate Golden Time as an ideal whole-school incentives and sanctions system. The loss of Golden Time is a very effective consequence for most children. Golden Time is a whole-school celebration for all the children who have kept the school's values for a week. We call these values our Golden Rules. Golden Time is normally an hour each week when work stops and each child who has kept the rules can take part in special exciting activities. Golden Time reinforces the expectation that children will keep the rules for the week and arrive at Golden Time with all their time intact. For those who break the rules there are systems whereby they can earn back some of their lost Golden Time, depending on the severity of their offence. For full details of how to operate Golden Time see Mosley and Sonnet, *Better Behaviour through Golden Time* (2005) in the Resources section.

REFLECT

Is our sanctions system effective? Do all members of staff know about it and how to apply it?

Where Golden Time is part of the school's incentives and sanctions system, loss of specified time can be incorporated into its consequences scheme (see page 36).

If a child loses five or ten minutes of their Golden Time, they sit with a five-minute sand timer when Golden Time begins. The timer is turned the necessary amount of times for the time lost. Once the time has been completed, the child is able to join in with a Golden Time activity of their choice. It is important that the child sits near the activity that they would have been doing had they not made a poor choice when they chose to act in a bullying manner, or to break the school's values in another way.

An important component of the consequences of a clear transgression against the school values, including an incident of bullying, is for the transgressor to fill in a Looking at my actions form (see page 37). Where possible, the child should be encouraged to fill this in on their own as it gives them an opportunity to consider their actions, the outcomes and how they might behave differently in future.

 A consequence has not been completed if a child fails to fill in this form satisfactorily. A hurried scribble, just to finish the task, will not suffice. Clearly explain to the child beforehand that the form is important. Help can be given in the form of gentle prompts, but don't ask leading questions – the child needs to think of their own answers.

An example of a set of consequences

The following table is an example of a set of consequences that could be used for bullying behaviour or behaviour that may lead to bullying. This could be used as the starting point for your school to develop their own agreed set of consequences.

Incident	First instance (potential bullying)	Second instance	Multiple instances
Indirect bullying: ostracising, spreading rumours, unpleasant comments, dismissive glances	Verbal warning and reminder of school rules	Time out or loss of Golden Time (see page 35)	Extended time out and loss of Golden Time, complete a Looking at my actions form, develop an Individual action plan (see page 39)
Direct bullying: spitting, pushing, tripping, violent threats, throwing objects, taking or damaging someone's property	Time out or loss of Golden Time, complete a Looking at my actions form	Extended time out and loss of Golden Time, complete a Looking at my actions form	Lesson-only contact with class for one week*, develop an Individual action plan
More violent direct bullying: hair pulling, punching, kicking	Extended time out, complete a Looking at my actions form	Lesson-only contact with class for one week*	Develop an Individual action plan

*The child must remain under adult supervision during playtimes.

Acts of extreme violence towards another person should automatically result in a period of exclusion from the school. For procedures for this you should refer to the policy for exclusion of your school and LEA.

Time out is intended as a period for reflection rather than a detention, and should be conveyed as such to the child. Make sure that there is no hidden reward for a child in the consequence they receive. Their time out should be carried out in silence under the supervision of an adult. The adult should not engage with a child during such a time, otherwise they might see this as an opportunity for gaining attention, negative attention being better than no attention at all.

LOOKING AT MY ACTIONS

What did I do? Draw and write your actions.

Why did I do this?

What could I have done differently?

Dealing with incidents

A good maxim is to strike while the iron is cold! In other words, be aware of the children who have the potential to become involved in bullying and praise them when you see them behaving well. Such pre-emptive action can have a significant impact on those children who need and seek attention. If they begin to feel that they get the attention they crave for good behaviour, they are much more likely to continue to seek this rather than putting their energy into getting attention through disruptive or bullying behaviour.

When you are dealing with children who have committed an act of bullying, there are several stages that they typically go through. The first of these could be denial. They may claim that they have done nothing. It is important that you remain calm and don't allow frustration or a feeling of helplessness to give rise to anger. Anger could lead you to over-react and say or do things that you later regret. Moreover, some children may have learnt that provoking an adult to anger may distract them from their intended outcome. Other children feed off the anger of others and unwittingly seek to provoke it. Speak in a neutral tone of voice and avoid a power struggle. If you are not getting the response you want, try again later. If you are confident about the reports regarding this child's behaviour, continue to repeat the question 'What did you do?' gently until the child acknowledges their actions or part in an incident.

The second stage a child may go through is blaming others for their actions. The child may

claim they only reacted because of provocation from others or because someone told them to. Do not involve any other children in the discussion. You can tell the child that you will deal with anyone else's behaviour at a later time (and make sure that you do, if it is warranted), but at the present you just want to concentrate on their actions.

The child may then attempt to minimise their actions, for example:

'I only tapped him.'
'I only said it once.'
'I accidentally knocked them over.'
'I didn't mean to push them.'

Ask children to repeat their statement, removing words such as 'just', 'only', 'accidentally' and 'might have'. When they say exactly what they have done without trying to qualify it, children are beginning to take responsibility for their actions.

Accepting responsibility means that children can accept the consequences of their actions, even if they have not yet developed empathy for the targeted child. They realise that if they perform certain actions, there will be a negative outcome for themselves and this will be inevitable.

Talking to children in specific terms about their actions and about the effects their actions had on others will help children towards the final stage of accepting that their actions make others unhappy. If children say they don't know if they have hurt someone, ask them to tell you how the child reacted – for example, by crying, running away, pulling a sad face.

You need to help children realise that they are not receiving consequences just because they have broken a rule or done something wrong. The rules serve a purpose – to protect people from being hurt physically or emotionally.

An important part of the consequence of bullying is for the child doing the bullying to reflect on their actions by filling in a Looking at my actions sheet. They should be helped to fill this in with specific detail such as 'I kicked

Joel and pushed him' rather than 'I was horrid to Joel.' Looking at the details of their actions helps them to understand what their motives are and how they can fulfil their needs in a more positive way.

ACTION PLAN

Would a child who bullies in your class benefit from working in a small circle or support group that focuses on enhancing self-esteem and developing the child's social skills?

Forming an action plan

When an Individual action plan has to be put in place, the parents of the child involved should be invited in to give their views and suggestions right from the beginning.

Key points to help you:

- Remember that the child who bullies is using negative strategies to fulfil needs – we don't believe people are bullies by nature.

- Identify the goals of their behaviour and look for more positive ways of achieving them.

- Maintain a positive regard for the child, don't show dislike of them.

- If they still have lapses of behaviour, don't negate any previous efforts.

- Encourage a positive belief that change is possible as well as desirable.

- Explore activities that will enhance the child's self-esteem and self-image.

- Try to give specific praise as this is more effective – for example, 'You stayed calm when Jodie pulled a mean face at you', rather than 'You've done really well today.'

- Commend them for being truthful when they own up to any misdemeanour. Give stickers and compliment slips for honesty (see Resources).

- Ask the child to focus on how they feel (e.g. disappointed), rather than telling them that you are sad when they do something negative – keep the focus on their actions.

- Use considered seating arrangements in class to allow responsible children to exert a positive influence and model good behaviour.

- Find out what motivates the child, and use a desirable reward along with descriptive praise to acknowledge both the progress made and the huge effort it takes to change.

There is a photocopiable action plan on page 41.

REFLECT

Would it help a child to be part of a lunchtime task force – a carefully selected small group (including good role models) that performs useful actions, such as renovating donated furniture under the supervision of a volunteer? At lunchtime it is best to keep the child so busy that they don't have time to get into trouble.

When you are setting a target for an action plan, be specific about the behaviours that you want to encourage or discourage. 'I will try to be good/kind' is too vague. Instead, put down exactly what you would like the child to do: 'I will try to walk away if someone says anything to me that I don't like' or 'I will try to stay away from the area at the side of the school.'

INDIVIDUAL ACTION PLAN

Name: ....

Class: ....

Date: ....

I will try to ....

....

....

I will try not to ....

....

....

If I get .... smiley faces this week my reward will be ....

....

....

Monday   **Tuesday**   **Wednesday**   **Thursday**   **Friday**

Signed

Child: ....   Teacher: ....

Likewise, be specific in the wording of behaviours you want the child to desist from – 'I will try not to kick or punch another child' or 'I will try not to call anyone a nasty name.'

Formulating an action plan provides a good opportunity for you to work closely with a child's parents. Acknowledge that you appreciate that they are doing the best they can for their child and commend them on all the positive things that they are managing to achieve. Asking them for their advice and input will show them that you are willing to work as a team with them, rather than against them and their child. If they support the actions you are taking, they will be more likely to contribute to the effort at home as well.

Be realistic when you set the target for the child to achieve. You want them to succeed and to be encouraged that they are able to change. If you set them up continually for failure, they will quickly become demoralised and discouraged from further effort.

Ensure that the reward you offer them for their effort is attractive and worthwhile. Allowing them to select a benefit such as a circle game for the whole class is a good incentive. If these children can create a treat for everyone with their good behaviour, there will be no incentive to the other children to wind the child up. They get a more positive reward by helping the child to be good. Discuss the reward with the child to find something they would really like. It is a good idea to change the reward every couple of weeks so that it retains its motivational value.

STRAND 4 – helping the child being bullied

Perhaps one of the most erroneous pieces of advice we can give to a child who is a target of bullying is to ignore the child doing the bullying and they will go away. This is not the case. Silence never works – it gives those who choose to bully the safety to continue hurting others without the fear of consequences.

Before giving any advice to a child who is bullied, you must actively listen to what they tell you. They may have tried a variety of different tactics such as walking away, being assertive, telling the child doing the bullying that their actions are hurtful, all to no avail. When these children try various methods without success, they feel completely helpless.

Moreover, in an environment where other children stand by and watch their suffering without offering to help or showing them sympathy, they may feel that they deserve to be bullied.

It would be wrong to minimise the effects that bullying may have on children. They may be very frightened by the real or perceived threats. They may become anxious, depressed and even suicidal, and the effects may last into adulthood. Children may suffer from psychosomatic illness or invent problems to stay away from school, and their learning can be seriously disrupted. If they feel that they in some way deserve the bullying and are worthless, they may experience problems associated with low self-esteem.

First and foremost, a targeted child needs to be protected from further harm and encouraged to talk to an adult. Children are often reluctant to tell because they may be picked on even more by the child doing the bullying, or because they don't want to be seen as a tell-tale. If your school actively promotes reporting such incidents as the correct response to bullying, there is less chance that a child will be seen as telling tales by other children.

A targeted child may be reluctant to tell an adult if they do not think they will get the help they require. Always make every effort to protect children at risk, otherwise they will stop reporting incidents. If a child finds it

ACTION PLAN

Watch a recorded TV programme or video/DVD that shows a bullying incident. Talk it through with the child, giving a particular emphasis to the fact that it is not the fault of the child being bullied that they are being treated in this way.

hard to approach adults, they can be given a mentor – a sensible trustworthy child – to talk to the adult on their behalf.

If you do offer advice, this should be given on a problem-solving basis – that is, if it is not effective, they can discard it and try something else. Remember that each disappointing outcome may add to their sense of failure.

It may be that you have little sympathy with a target of bullying because they behave in a provocative way or they over-react to incidents. However, this should not influence your effort to protect them. Children who provoke others to react may not know a more positive way of getting attention from their peers. In addition to the protection you offer them, they too may need consequences in order to deter them from certain behaviours and encouragement to seek attention in a less negative way.

Children who react are often seen as easy prey and a constant source of entertainment for those involved in bullying because of their extreme responses. These children may have learnt that their tears gain them the sympathy and attention of adults or they may be overly cosseted at home. Reactive children often feel and say that no-one cares about them. Even though you may consider that what they are

ACTION PLAN

If a child is in immediate danger, could you give them responsible jobs during playtime that will keep them safe and raise their self-esteem?

telling you is unrealistic, this is their perception of their lives. You can help these children by not being too sympathetic or dwelling on their misfortune. Talk to them about all the positive things in their lives and all the kind children in their class, and try to help them to build a little more self-confidence.

Providing a targeted child with a Circle of Support can be a helpful approach. This is a group of trustworthy and caring children who are asked to play with the child during break times. Explain to them that the child may be uncooperative at times and difficult to get along with, but you are asking them to try their hardest to help by encouraging them to join in their games. This often helps to increase other children's tolerance and understanding of the child in question, while enhancing their relationships and developing inclusion.

A carefully planned programme of games and activities can help the functioning of this group.

With older children, you may like to try a support group for the target child that includes the child doing the bullying and some of the bystanders. All the members of the group, including the targeted child, take joint responsibility for finding a solution. The children are encouraged to adopt a problem-solving method, not a blaming approach. Each participant should be interviewed separately after one week to check on progress, and the group must be monitored regularly to assess its effectiveness.

The most important issue is that targets of bullying know that you will keep them safe from further harm.

STRAND 5 – working with parents

If you want to help the children in your school, you must try to develop good relationships with their parents.

When you have an induction evening for new children and parents, you can explain the school's policy on anti-bullying. This is a good opportunity to convey to parents the pride you feel in an anti-bullying ethos that aims to provide an environment in which everyone can feel safe, physically and emotionally. They will be expected to support this approach and become familiar with the methods and strategies that you use to uphold it.

You can encourage parents to share any concerns that they might have about their children's welfare with members of staff, and assure them that you will listen and take any action that is necessary to maintain the high standards you expect from the children in your school.

If a parent reports an incident of bullying to the school, it is vital that you act upon it. Even if your view is that the parent is being overprotective, you must be seen to follow up every complaint. It is a good idea to ask the parents to write down the specific details of incidents – when, where and exactly what they believed happened.

Remember, it is difficult for some parents to come into school and talk to teachers. They may have negative views from their own school days and distrust teachers in general. They may feel that staff discriminate against their child and do not like them.

Useful tips for working with parents

- Always welcome parents into school and show that you are pleased to see them.

- Talk about their child in a positive tone of voice, even when making a complaint about their behaviour.

- Invite parents to join you for Golden Time and specific Circle Times to help them understand these systems.

- Use a problem-solving rather than a blaming approach.

- Acknowledge the good work that parents do – they may be struggling with the child at home as well.

- Ask parents for their views and advice. Enlisting them as team members is important.

- Even though you may disagree with their parenting style, remember that most people are doing their best for their children.

- Work with the parents and help them with suggestions about what they could do at home – for example, giving rewards for good behaviour, showing children more positive ways to get what they want, encouraging family members to model good behaviour.

- If you reach stalemate in your discussions, ask the parents what they would like the school to do in specific terms. Don't respond to their anger with anger. You may not be able to commit to it all, but it gives you a basis for discussion and negotiation.

- Meet regularly with the parents so that you can tell them of progress made, not just when you have bad news to report.

- Obtaining the goodwill and support of parents is important. You are far more likely to succeed in your aims if you work together.

- Bring in outside agencies to support parents where appropriate.

REFLECT

The most important aspect of dealing with parents is to remain non-judgemental.

CONCLUSION

'Culture' is the word we use to describe the way in which life is lived by groups of people. When we talk about culture, we are talking about the beliefs and rules that drive people's actions and how they behave towards one another. Every school is a community with its own particular culture that determines whether the school is successful and happy, or struggling and fretful. Paying attention to the culture that pervades your school is probably the most significant factor in everything you do.

We must all ask ourselves who wields the cultural power in our school. If you ignore instances of bullying and hope they will go away, you are allowing the least healthy members of your community to have the power to build the culture of your school. When bullying becomes rife, a school is prey to developing a culture of fear, secrecy, distrust and defensive self-protection that can infiltrate every aspect of how it functions. You cannot allow that to happen. You, the adults in your school community, have the role of builders of its culture. You will have the power to make it dynamic and productive if you set about ensuring that bullying is put where it belongs – as far away as possible from your school.

This book has explained how to build a culture that shows children (and staff) that each of them is valued because pro-social behaviour is consistently encouraged and rewarded. You have the power to eradicate the anxious secrecy that bullying creates and to cultivate a 'telling' environment in which the voices of victims – and of the quiet majority of observers – are heard and everyone understands that the maintenance of a safe school is a responsibility shared by every member of the community.

You have learnt how to construct a favourable culture by utilising the strategies at your disposal. These include making sure that everyone understands exactly what bullying is and how it will be treated in your school; how to adapt the curriculum so that discussion can take place and everyone feels that their voice is heard; and how to deal with perpetrators, targets and parents. The time and effort you put into making your school a physically and emotionally safe place mean that you are building a culture that has integrity.

If you use the strategies in this book, you will be helping your children to become adaptable, productive and successful adults. Now you have reached the end, assess your progress by completing the checklist on page 47.

KEEPING YOUR HELP EFFECTIVE

Consider the following questions to see where you need to focus in your action plan.

1. Is your anti-bullying policy up to date and effective? **Yes No**

2. Do all members of the school community know the correct procedures for dealing with bullying incidents? **Yes No**

3. Do you have an effective whole-school incentives and sanctions system in operation, such as Golden Time? **Yes No**

4. Are the children in your class able to say what bullying is? **Yes No**

5. Do the children in your class understand how witnesses can affect a situation, and can they outline the proper course of action? **Yes No**

6. Are the measures that you use with children involved in bullying producing a positive effect on their behaviour? **Yes No**

7. Are you satisfied that children who are bullied know how to obtain help, and that they trust it will be effective? **Yes No**

8. Do you believe that you enjoy positive relationships with the parents of all the children in your class? **Yes No**

RESOURCES

Mosley, J. (1993) *Turn your School Round*
Mosley, J. (1996) *Quality Circle Time*
Mosley, J. (1998) *More Quality Circle Time*
Mosley, J. and Sonnet, H. (2002) *101 Games for Self-Esteem*
Mosley, J. and Sonnet, H. (2002) *Making Waves*
Mosley, J. and Sonnet, H. (2003) *101 Games for Social Skills*
Mosley, J. and Sonnet, H. (2005) *Better Behaviour through Golden Time*
Mosley, J. and Sonnet, H. (2006) *101 Games for Better Behaviour*
Mosley, J. and Sonnet, H. (2006) *Using Rewards Wisely*
Mosley, J. and Thorp, G. (2005) *Positive Playtimes*

Mosley, J. (2000) *Quality Circle Time in Action*
Mosley, J. (2000) *Quality Circle Time Kit*
Mosley, J. (2004) *Reward Certificates*
Mosley, J. (2004) *Stickers*
Mosley, J. (2005) *Golden Rules Poster*
Mosley, J. (2005) *Playground Stars*

All these resources are published in Cambridge by LDA. For information about the full range of Jenny Mosley's books and resources, please contact LDA Customer Services on 0845 120 4776 or visit our website at www.LDAlearning.com

Training in the Quality Circle Time model

For information about training, contact Jenny Mosley Consultancies:
Telephone: 01225 767157
E-mail: circletime@jennymosley.co.uk
Website: www.circle-time.co.uk
Address: 28a Gloucester Road, Trowbridge, Wiltshire, BA14 0AA

Sources of information

Alexander, J. (1998) *Your Child Bullying: Practical and Easy to Follow Advice*. Element Books
DfES (2003) *Bullying – Don't Suffer in Silence*
DfES (2005) *Excellence and Enjoyment: Social and Emotional Aspects of Learning*
Kidscape (1990) *Keeping Safe: A Practical Guide to Talking with Children*. Kidscape (152 Buckingham Palace Road, London, SW1W 9TR)
Mellor, A. (1993) *Bullying and how to Fight it: A Guide for Families*. Scottish Council for Research in Education (15 St John Street, Edinburgh, EH5 5JR)

Organisations

Anti-Bullying Alliance, National Children's Bureau, 8 Wakley Street, London, EC1V 7QE
Anti-Bullying Network, Moray House School of Education, University of Edinburgh, Holyrood Road, Edinburgh, EH8 8AQ
Parentline Plus, 520 Highgate Studios, 53–79 Highgate Road, Kentish Town, London, NW5 1TL

Useful websites

www.antibullying.net
www.anti-bullyingalliance.org
www.bullying.co.uk
www.childline.org.uk
www.dfes.gov.uk/bullying
www.kidscape.org.uk
www.parentlineplus.org.uk